A short introduction to the Danish language, for the use of those who choose to learn it in a methodical way.

A short introduction to the Danish language, for the use of those who choose to learn it in a methodical way.
Multiple Contributors, See Notes
ESTCID: T132715
Reproduction from British Library
With a final errata and advertisement leaf.
London : printed by R. Hilton, 1774.
66,[2]p. ; 8°

Gale ECCO Print Editions

Relive history with *Eighteenth Century Collections Online,* now available in print for the independent historian and collector. This series includes the most significant English-language and foreign-language works printed in Great Britain during the eighteenth century, and is organized in seven different subject areas including literature and language; medicine, science, and technology; and religion and philosophy. The collection also includes thousands of important works from the Americas.

The eighteenth century has been called "The Age of Enlightenment." It was a period of rapid advance in print culture and publishing, in world exploration, and in the rapid growth of science and technology – all of which had a profound impact on the political and cultural landscape. At the end of the century the American Revolution, French Revolution and Industrial Revolution, perhaps three of the most significant events in modern history, set in motion developments that eventually dominated world political, economic, and social life.

In a groundbreaking effort, Gale initiated a revolution of its own: digitization of epic proportions to preserve these invaluable works in the largest online archive of its kind. Contributions from major world libraries constitute over 175,000 original printed works. Scanned images of the actual pages, rather than transcriptions, recreate the works *as they first appeared.*

Now for the first time, these high-quality digital scans of original works are available via print-on-demand, making them readily accessible to libraries, students, independent scholars, and readers of all ages.

For our initial release we have created seven robust collections to form one the world's most comprehensive catalogs of 18th century works.

Initial Gale ECCO Print Editions collections include:

History and Geography
Rich in titles on English life and social history, this collection spans the world as it was known to eighteenth-century historians and explorers. Titles include a wealth of travel accounts and diaries, histories of nations from throughout the world, and maps and charts of a world that was still being discovered. Students of the War of American Independence will find fascinating accounts from the British side of conflict.

Social Science
Delve into what it was like to live during the eighteenth century by reading the first-hand accounts of everyday people, including city dwellers and farmers, businessmen and bankers, artisans and merchants, artists and their patrons, politicians and their constituents. Original texts make the American, French, and Industrial revolutions vividly contemporary.

Medicine, Science and Technology
Medical theory and practice of the 1700s developed rapidly, as is evidenced by the extensive collection, which includes descriptions of diseases, their conditions, and treatments. Books on science and technology, agriculture, military technology, natural philosophy, even cookbooks, are all contained here.

Literature and Language
Western literary study flows out of eighteenth-century works by Alexander Pope, Daniel Defoe, Henry Fielding, Frances Burney, Denis Diderot, Johann Gottfried Herder, Johann Wolfgang von Goethe, and others. Experience the birth of the modern novel, or compare the development of language using dictionaries and grammar discourses.

Religion and Philosophy
The Age of Enlightenment profoundly enriched religious and philosophical understanding and continues to influence present-day thinking. Works collected here include masterpieces by David Hume, Immanuel Kant, and Jean-Jacques Rousseau, as well as religious sermons and moral debates on the issues of the day, such as the slave trade. The Age of Reason saw conflict between Protestantism and Catholicism transformed into one between faith and logic -- a debate that continues in the twenty-first century.

Law and Reference
This collection reveals the history of English common law and Empire law in a vastly changing world of British expansion. Dominating the legal field is the *Commentaries of the Law of England* by Sir William Blackstone, which first appeared in 1765. Reference works such as almanacs and catalogues continue to educate us by revealing the day-to-day workings of society.

Fine Arts
The eighteenth-century fascination with Greek and Roman antiquity followed the systematic excavation of the ruins at Pompeii and Herculaneum in southern Italy; and after 1750 a neoclassical style dominated all artistic fields. The titles here trace developments in mostly English-language works on painting, sculpture, architecture, music, theater, and other disciplines. Instructional works on musical instruments, catalogs of art objects, comic operas, and more are also included.

The BiblioLife Network

This project was made possible in part by the BiblioLife Network (BLN), a project aimed at addressing some of the huge challenges facing book preservationists around the world. The BLN includes libraries, library networks, archives, subject matter experts, online communities and library service providers. We believe every book ever published should be available as a high-quality print reproduction; printed on-demand anywhere in the world. This insures the ongoing accessibility of the content and helps generate sustainable revenue for the libraries and organizations that work to preserve these important materials.

The following book is in the "public domain" and represents an authentic reproduction of the text as printed by the original publisher. While we have attempted to accurately maintain the integrity of the original work, there are sometimes problems with the original work or the micro-film from which the books were digitized. This can result in minor errors in reproduction. Possible imperfections include missing and blurred pages, poor pictures, markings and other reproduction issues beyond our control. Because this work is culturally important, we have made it available as part of our commitment to protecting, preserving, and promoting the world's literature.

GUIDE TO FOLD-OUTS MAPS and OVERSIZED IMAGES

The book you are reading was digitized from microfilm captured over the past thirty to forty years. Years after the creation of the original microfilm, the book was converted to digital files and made available in an online database.

In an online database, page images do not need to conform to the size restrictions found in a printed book. When converting these images back into a printed bound book, the page sizes are standardized in ways that maintain the detail of the original. For large images, such as fold-out maps, the original page image is split into two or more pages

Guidelines used to determine how to split the page image follows:

• Some images are split vertically; large images require vertical and horizontal splits.
• For horizontal splits, the content is split left to right.
• For vertical splits, the content is split from top to bottom.
• For both vertical and horizontal splits, the image is processed from top left to bottom right.

A SHORT
INTRODUCTION
TO THE
Danish Language,
FOR THE
U S E
OF.
Those who choose to learn it in a methodical
W A Y.

LONDON:
Printed by R. HILTON, No. 8, Wellclose Square,
M,DCC,LXXIV.

The DANES have 27 Letters in their Alphabet, whose Names you will observe

thus A	a and are sounded as	A
B	b	Fe
C	c	Ce
D	d	De
E	e	E
F	f	eF
G	g	Ge
H	h	Haa
I	i	I
K	k	Kaa
L	l	eL
M	m	eM
N	n	eN
O	o	O
P	p	Pe
Q	q	Q
R	r	eR
S	s	eS
T	t	Te
U	u	U
V	v	Ve
W	w	
X	x	eX
Y	y	Y
Z	z	Zetta
Æ	æ	a e
Ö	o	Ö

A SHORT INTRODUCTION TO THE Danish Language.

§ 1. EVERY letter retains its own natural sound, without any alteration in their composition of words, or in their pronunciation.

§ 2. In the Danish language you will observe the same articles as in English, viz.

1. The INDIFINITE or the Article of Unity.
2. The DEFINITIVE ARTICLE.

§ 3. The Indifinite Article of Unity is
EN *or* ET *as* en Mand, *a man.*
ET *One, as* et Bord, *a table.*

§ 4 The Definitive Article.
Den *or* Det, which answers to the English *the*, as

Den Hest, *the Horse.*

And it is again divided into
1 The PREPOSITIVE
2 The POSTPOSITIVE

§ 5 The Prepositive stands before Definitive Words and is call'd Den *or* Det, *The*

Singular	Plural
Det Barn *the child*	De Born *the children*
Den Jomfru *the lady*	De Jomfruer *the ladies*

§ 6 The Postpositive EN and ET, when used definitively is always put at the end of words, and likewise answers to the English *the*, as

Singular	Plural
Jomfruen *the lady*	Jomfruene *the ladies*
Barnet *the child*	Bornene *the children*

§ 7. The definitive articles have two numbers.

Singular	Plural
En *or* Et	Ene
Den *and* Det	De

§ 8. Any word ending in a consonant as

et Bord *a table*

puts the article behind, when the word becomes definitve, as

Singular.	Plural.
Bordet *the table*	Bordene *the tables*
Hesten *the horse*	Hestene *the horses*
Manden *the man*	Mændene *the man*

§ 9 When the word ends in a vowel, the E of the second article prepositive EN, looses its E, as

en Kaarde *a sword*   Kaarden *the sword*
en Troe *a faith*   Troen *the faith*

en

et Bytte *a prey*   Byttet *the prey*

et Oye *an eye*   Oyet *the eyes*

§ 10. The articles have two genders, which may be called, the first, PRIUS, and the second POSTERIUS

Note 1. Prius is both masculine and feminine. The article stands before the nouns of either kind.

Note 2. Posterius is more like the neuter gender, though it often comprehends the common gender, and sometimes only masculine and feminine.

§ 11. The Article of unity hath
    1 Gen. Prius   en   *a*
    2   Posterius et   *one*

THE DEFINITIVE ARTICLE.
1st. Prepositive.

§ 12. The first gender hath prius.
   Sing. Den *the*   Den Mand *the man*
   Plur. De *the*   De Mænd *the men*

§ 13. 2nd. Gender posterius.
   Sing. Det *the*   Det Bord , *the table*
   Plur. De *the*   De Bord *the table*

2. Postpositive.

§ 14. First gender hath prius.
     Sing. en *the man* Manden
     Plur. ene *the men* Mændene.

§ 15. Second gender hath posterius.
   Sing et *a or one*.   Plur ene
   Brodet *the loaf*   Brodene *the loaves*

§ 16. The Nouns are of several kinds, but we shall confine them to the two following, viz.

SUBSTANTIVES *and* ADJECTIVES, which are alike in all languages.

§ 17. The cases of declension are as in the English six, but none of them alter the termination, except the genitive, which is formed by adding *s*, as in the

Indefinite Sense
Man *Gen.* Mands.
Brod   Brods.

With the definite postpositive article
Manden *Gen.* Mandens.
Brodet   Brodets.

Of the GENDERS.

§ 18. The Danes (as before observed) have two genders, the same as the articles and of the same name.

§ 19. 1 Prius, which is known by the article EN, *A*, as

Singular		Plural	
en Stoel	*a chair*	Stole	*chairs*
en Siæl	*a soul*	Siæle	*souls*
en Ford	*an earth*	Iorde	*earths*
en Engel	*an angel*	Engel	*angels*

§ 20. 2. Posterius, known by the article ET, *One*, as

Singular		Plural	
et Ægg	*an egg*	Æggene	*the eggs*
et Aar	*a year*	Aaret	*the years*
et Bryst	*a breast*	Brystet	*the breasts*

En

To the DANISH LANGUAGE.

§ 21. The most nouns are of the first gender or prius.

§ 22. Of the second, or Posterius, we will observe the following collection of words, which when learned by heart, will enable you to find the remainder of this kind, that have no particular rule, but the idiom of the language.

ET		
	Ægteskab	Wedlock, Marriage
	Ærm	Sleeve
	Affald	Drofs, Defertion
	Affskum	Scum
	Affslag	Refusal, Abatement
	Alter	Altar
	Anker	Anchor
	Anlob	Concourfe
	Anflag	Advice, Direction
	Anstod	Offence, Stumbling-block
	Andtal	Number, Multitude
	Apotheque	Apothecary's Shop
	Arbeide	Work, Labour
	Ark-papir	Sheet of Paper
	Afen	Afs
	Ar	Scar
	Ax	Ear
	Aadsel	Carcafe
	Aag	Yoke
	Aar	Year
	Aasyn	Countenance
	Allun	Allum
	Æmbede	Office
	Anskrig	Cry, Shout
	Ansight	Face
	Archiv	Archives

ET Baand

ET Baand   A *Bandage*
   Bad   *Bath*
   Bendel   *Tape*
   Banquet   *Banquet*
   Barn   *Child*
   Baghold   *Retreat*
   Belte   *Girdle, Belt*
   Baronic   *Barons Estate*
   Bedrag   *Fraud*
   Bedragerie   *Cheat, Deceit*
   Been   *Bone, a Man's Leg*
   Bæger   *Cup, Mug*
   Begreb   *Skill, Judgment, Ingenuity*
   Behag   *Pleasure*
   Behold   *Remainder, Rest*
   Beslag   *Furniture, Cover*
   Beviis   *Witness, Receipt*
   Bibliotheque   *Library*
   Bid   *Bite*
   Bidsel   *Bridle*
   Bierg   *Mountain*
   Biefald   *Consent*
   Bind   *Bindings, Stock*
   Bindsel   *Bandage*
   Blink   *Flash of Light*
   Blomster   *Flower*
   Bluss   *Flambeau, a Flame*
   Bogstav   *Letter*
   Bolerie   *Buggery, Sodomy*
   Bord   *Table*
   Borgeskab   *Freedom, Privilege of a Corporation*
   Borr   *Gimblet*
   Brev   *Letter*
   Brygerie   *Brewery*

ET Brylup

To the DANISH LANGUAGE.

ET	Bryllup	A	*Wedding*
	Bryst		*Breast*
	Bud		*Commandment, Message*
	Budskab		*Message*
	Bugt		*Creek, Bay*
	Bytte		*Prey*
	Best		*Beast*
	Beg		*Pitch*
	Bekken		*Bason, Dish*
	Billed		*Image*
	Bispedom		*Bishoprick*
	Blad		*Leaf, Blade*
	Bogskab		*Book-case*
	Boeskab		*Furniture*
	Blod		*Blood*
	Bræt		*Board*
	Brod		*Bread*
	Bryggerhuus		*Brewhouse*
	Bundt		*Bundle*

ET	Cameradskab	A	*Fellowship*
	Cancellie		*Chancery*
	Chor		*Choir*
	Compagnie		*Company*
	Creatur		*Creature*
	Contoir		*Countinghouse*
	Castel		*Castle*
	Claveer		*Virginals*
	Clysteer		*Glyster*
	Capell		*Chapel*

ET	Dekken	A	*Blanket, Counterpane*
	Drog		*Drone*
	Dyr		*Deer*
	Dyn		*Puddle, Quagmire*

ET Exempel

12 A Short INTRODUCTION

ET Exempel — Example
Embede — Office

Fad — A Dish
Fakkel — Touch
Fald — Fall
Fongsel — Prison
Fiendskab — Enmity
Flor — Crape, Gauze
Folgeskab — Company in Walking
Forbund — Bond, Agreement, Society
Forhæng — Curtain
Foedklæde — Carpet
Forklæde — Apron
Forsæt — Design, Proposal, Decree
Forvandskab — Kindred, Relationship
Foster — Infant
Fyrsted — Fireplace
Fag — Small Squares (in Building) or Frames

Faar — Sheep
Fæe — Cattle
Fæste — Handle, Hilt, Lease
Forhor — Hearing, Examination
Folk — People
Foll — Colt
Fodder — Hay, Fodder
Forgist — Poison
Fortoüg — Foot-path
Fuglebur — Cage
Fyztoy — Tinder Box
Fruentimer — Woman

Gab — A Gap, Aperture
Gardin — Curtain

ET Gain

To the DANISH LANGUAGE.

ET	Garn	A	Worsted, Net
	Gavn		Advantage, Emolument Benefit
	Giærde		Hedge
	Giftermaal		Marriage
	Gilde		Feast
	Gibs		Plaister of Paris, Stocco Work
	Grævskab		Earldom
	Gehæng		Sword Belt
	Gemak		Chamber, Apartment
	Gemyt		Mind
	Gidsel		Sponsor, Pledge
	Glas		Glass
	Gods		Goods
	Græs		Grass
	Guld		Gold
	Gulv		Floor

ET	Haab	A	Hope
	Had		Hatred
	Harnish		Armour
	Helbred		Health
	Helvede		Hell
	Hensigt		Respect
	Herred		Manor
	Herskab		Lordship
	Hiorne		Corner of a Street, or House
	Hoved		Head
	Hug		Cut
	Hæfte		Hilt
	Haar		Hair
	Harpix		Rosin
	Hav		Ocean
	Hierte		Heart

C ET

ET Hiul | A Wheel
Horn | Horn
Hofpital | Hofpital
Hul | Hole
Hüüs | Houfe
Hoe | Hay

ET Iein | A Iron
Iver | Dug
Ifter | Greafe, Lard
Infantery | Infantry

ET Kald | A Calling
Kamer | Room
Kaar | Choice, Condition
Kar | Tub, Veffel
Kaft | Throw, Caft
Klæde | Cloth
Kloft | Breach, Gap
Kiokken | Kitchen
Küll | Coal
Kys | Kifs, Salute by Lips
Kaaber | Copper
Kors | Crofs
Kallun | Tripe
Keyferdom | Empire
Kid | Kid
Kiod | Flefh
Kladerie | Scribble
Klenodie | Prize
Klofter | Cloifter
Knæe | Knee
Knal | Sound, Report
Knippe | Bunch
Korn | Corn, Grain
Krud | Gun Powder

ET Kiar

To the DANISH LANGUAGE. 15

ET Kiær   A *Pond, Pale*
    Krŭŭs   *Tankard*

ET Laag   A *Pot-Lid*
    Laar   *Thigh*
    Laug   *Society*
    Legeme   *Body*
    Liverie   *Livery*
    Liig   *Corps*
    Linned   *Linen*
    Lob   *Course, Run*
    Lofte   *Promise*
    Loft   *Loft*
    Læder   *Leather*
    Lam   *Lamb*
    Las   *Load*
    Lem   *Member*
    Lehn   *Fee, Tenement*
    Liv   *Life, of the Soul*
    Levnet   *Life, Behaviour of Life*
    Ledemod   *Joint*
    Lod   *Share, Weight*
    Logement   *Lodgings*
    Lys   *Candle, Light*
    Lagen   *Sheet*

ET Maaltid   A *Meal*
    Maal   *Measure*
    Mærke   *Mark*
    Menneske   *Man*
    Moed   *Spirit, Courage*
    Mord   *Homicide, Murder*
    Meel   *Flower*
    Middel   *Means, Method*
    Miracle   *Miracle*

ET Mynster	A *Copy, Model*
Madskab	*Cupboard*
ET Neeg	A *Sheaf*
Nag	*Envy*
Navn	*Name*
Næmme	*Acuteness, Ingenuity*
ET Opror	A *Sedition, Rebellion*
Orgel	*Organ*
Orlog	*War at Sea*
Öyeblik	*Moment*
Oll	*Beer*
Öre	*Ear*
Öye	*Eye*
Offer	*Offering, Offer*
Oracle	*Oracle*
Oxhoved	*Hogshead*
Öyelaag	*Eyelid*
Opvext	*Growth*
ET Pálads	A *Palace*
Pass	*Passport*
Politie	*Policy*
Purpur	*Purple, Crimson*
Provstie	*Deanery*
Puds	*Trick*
Pandzer	*Armour*
Papir	*Paper*
Par	*Pair*
Pergament	*Parchment*
Plaster	*Plaister*
Pulpit	*Pulpit*
Pulpitur	*Gallery*
Pund	*Pound*

ET Plads

To the DANISH LANGUAGE. 17

ET Plads — A Place
    Paafund — Invention
    Pakhuus — Warehouse

ET Quarteer — A Quartern
    Quintin — One-8th of an Ounce

ET Raab — A Clamour, Voice, Schriek
    Raad — Advice
    Reeb — Rope
    Rus-papir — Rheam of Paper
    Redskab — Tools
    Register — Register
    Rige — Kingdom
    Rom — Room
    Rov — Prey, Robbery
    Rivejern — Grater
    Ris — Rod

ET Saar — A Sore, Ulcer
    Samenhæng — Connection
    Samfund — Communion
    Sæde — Seat
    Sælskab — Company, Society
    Salt — Salt
    Saltkar — Salt-sellers
    Sigt — Sight
    Sind — Mind
    Schaberaque
    Skiæg — Beard
    Skaar — Cut
    Skarn — Dross, Dirt
    Skiell — Shell
    Skind — Skin
    Skiold — Shield

ET Skiort

18 A Short INTRODUCTION

ET	Skiort	A *Pettycoat*
	Skiod	*Lap*
	Skridt	*Step*
	Skud	*Report of a Gun, Bud*
	Slag	*Stroke, Battle*
	Smor	*Butter*
	Som	*Nail*
	Spidt	*Spit*
	Sporsmaal	*Question*
	Sprog	*Language*
	Speil	*Looking Glass*
	Spyd	*Spear, Lance*
	Sted	*Place*
	Staal	*Steel*
	Stod	*Hurt*
	Stov	*Dust*
	Suk	*Sigh*
	Svelg	*Swallow, Whirlpool*
	Svar	*Answer*
	Sving	*Swing*
	Segel	*Seal*
	Seil	*Sail*
	Signet	*Signet*
	Schafot	*Scaffold*
	Skaft	*Handle*
	Skib	*Ship*
	Skierf	*Sash*
	Skildt	*Sign*
	Skilderie	*Picture*
	Skrog	*Skeleton, Bulk*
	Skrub	*Scrubing Brush*
	Skiul	*Shelter*
	Slot	*Palace*
	Sogn	*Parish*
	Solv	*Silver*

ET Spand

To the DANISH LANGUAGE.

ET Spand	A Pail
Spectacle	Play
Spill	Play, Game
Spogelse	Spectre
Spind	Invention, Trick
Stift	Bishoprick, Cathedral Church
Straae	Straw
Stræde	Lane
Stykke	Piece, Cannon
Sverd	Sword
Sviin	Swine, Hog
Syn	Sight, Apparition
Senge, Tepen	Quilt
Skiermbret	Skreen
Springvand	Fountain
Snoie, Liv	Stays
Sæt	Head-Dress, Cap
Stieboyle	Stirrup
ET Tag	A Roof
Talent	Talent, Gift
Tegn	Sign
Telt	Telt
Testament	Testament
Tin	Pewter
Toy	Toy
Træe	Tree
Træværk	Rails
Tab	Loss
Tall	Number
Tillæg	Addition
Tog	War
Torv	Market-Place
Trin	Step, Stair

ET Trug

20 A Short INTRODUCTION

ET Træg	A *Tray*
Tyranie	*Tyranny*
Tyverie	*Theft*
ET Udfald	A *Event*
Udskud	*Refuse*
Utoy	*Vermin*
Verse	*Verse, Rhyme*
Vidne	*Witness*
Vaaben	*Armour*
Vand	*Water*
Værk	*Work*
Væsen	*Essence, Substance*
Veyer	*Weather*
Vindow	*Window*

§ 23. When an Indefinite Noun, or a Noun without an Article, ends in a Consonant, it forms its Plural by adding E at the end, as

Singular		Plural	
Hest	*Horse*	Heste	*Horses*
Steen	*Stone*	Stene	*Stones*
Stoel	*Chair*	Stole	*Chairs*

§ 24 These following are formed by adding E R, as do most of the Posterius Gender.

Singular		Plural	
Dyd	*Virtue*	Dyder	*Virtue*
Plight	*a Duty*	Plighter	*Duties*
Hoved	*an Head*	Hoveder	*Heads*
Ansigt	*a Face*	Ansigter	*Faces*

§ 25. When

§ 25 When the Indefinite Noun ends in an E, it makes the Plural by adding R or ER, as

Singular		Plural	
Menneſke	*Man*	Menneſker	*Men*
Kirke	*Church*	Kirker	*Churches*
Frue	*Lady*	Fruer	*Ladies*

§ 26. Likewiſe when it ends in a Dipthong, or any other Vowel, as

Singular		Plural	
Aae	*River*	Aaer	*Rivers*
Træ	*Tree*	Træer	*Trees*
Bie	*Bee*	Bier	*Bees*
Omhue	*Care*	Omhuer	*Cares*
Moe	*Virgin*	Moer	*Virgins*

§ 27. All proper Nouns end their Plural in ER, as

Singular		Plural	
Hans	*John*	Hanſer	*Johns*
Wolff		Wolffer	
Jorgen	*George*	Jorgener	*Georges*
Elizabeth		Elizabether	

§ 28. The following Nouns, beſides forming their Plural according to the before-mentioned Rules, alſo change their Vowels; as A into Æ, and O into Ø, viz.

Sing.		Plur.
And	*Duck*	Ænder
Bog	*a Book*	Bøger
Bonde	*a Farmer*	Bønder

Sing.		Plur.
Bod	*Penitence*	Boder, Mulct, Fine
Dotter	*a Daughter*	Dottre
Fod	*a Foot*	Foder, Feet
Haand	*an Hand*	Hænder
Kloe	*a Claw*	Kloer
Nat	*a Night*	Nætter
Rand	*a Stripe*	Rænder
Rod	*a Root*	Roder
Soe	*a Sea*	Soer
Stand	*a State*	Stænder
Stang	*a Barr*	Stænger
Taae	*a Toe*	Tæer
Tand	*a Tooth*	Tænder
Tang	*a Tongue*	Tænger

§ 29. The following Nouns do not change their Termination in the Singular or Plural Number, without you prefix or annex the Definitive Article, DEN *or* DET, EN *or* ET, as

Aag	*Yoke*
Ark	*Sheet of Paper*
Brod	*Bread*
Bud	*Commandment*
Faar	*Sheep*
Fied	*Footstep*
Folk	*People*
Kull	*Coal*
Lam	*Lamb*
Liv	*Life*
Maik	*Maggots*
Moll	*Mote*
Neb	*Bill*

Nod

Nød	*Cattle*
Ord	*Word*
Raad	*Counsel*
Reeb	*Ropes*
Rips	*Currants*
Sild	*Herring*
Sind	*Mind*
Skind	*Skin*
Skridt	*Step*
Sviin	*Swine*
Tall	*Number*
Ting	*Thing*

§ 30. Some Nouns are quite irregular in the formation of their Plural, as

Sing		Plur.
Anden	*Other*	Andre
Barn	*Child*	Børn
Fader	*Father*	Fædre
Gaas	*Goose*	Giæs
Mangen	*Many*	Mange
Nogen	*Somebody*	Nogle
Ore	*Ear*	Oren
Oye	*Eye*	Oyen
Oxe	*Ox*	Oxen
Liden	*Little*	Smaae
Meget	*Much*	Mange

§ 31. The Plural Nouns in the Indefinite Sense are unaltered in a Definite Sense, adding the Postpositive Article to them, as

Børn	*Children*	Bornene	*the Children*
Giæs	*Geese*	Giæsene	*the Geese*
Fædre	*Parents*	Fædrene	*the Parents*

Fruer

24 A Short INTRODUCTION

| Fruer | *Ladies* | Fruerne | *the Ladies* |
| Læier | *Mosters* | Læierne | *the Masters* |

§ 32 When the Postpositive Article is added to the Plurals ending in R, it loses its first E, as

Fruer	*Ladies*	Fruer-ne	*the Ladies*
Ansigter	*Faces*	Ansigter-ne	*the Faces*
Æbler	*Apples*	Æbler-ne	*the Apples*

Of Adjectives.

§ 33. Adjectives are Words that signify the Quality of any Person, Place or Thing

Adjectives are always like Substantives in the Prius Gender, as

En god Mand	*A good Man*
En smuk Pige	*A pretty Girl*
En deilig Kone	*A handsome Wife*

But

§ 34 In the Posterius Gender they sometimes assume a T, as

Et god-t Huus	*A good House*
Et god-t Bord	*A good Table*
Et kostbar-t Fad	*A precious Dish or Vessel*
Et lang-t ansigt	*A long Face*
Et bred-t bryst	*A broad Breast*

§ 35 If an Adjective is joined with a Substantive that has the Definite Prepositive Article, it assumes an E, as

| Den Stock | *the Stick* |
| Den god-e Stock | *the good Stick* |

Den

Den Mand	*the Man*
Den høy-e Mand	*the tall Man*
Det Slot	*the Palace*
Det stor-e Slot	*the great Palace*

§ 36. If an Adjective stands before a Substantive of an Indefinite Sense, it likewise takes a T at the End, as

Dyrebar-t Rogelse	*Precious Frankincense*
Smuk-t Toy	*A pretty Toy*
Fiin-t Linned	*Fine Linen*

§ 37. Adjectives, and also Pronouns, ending in N, as Liden, Megen, Din, Min, Den, changes N into T before the Substantives of the Posterius Gender, as

Et Slot	*a Palace*
Et lidet Slot	*a little Palace*
Det Brod	*the Bread*
Det meget Brod	*that much Bread*
Et Ansigt	*a Face*
Mit Ansigt	*my Face*
Et Uhr	*a Watch*
Dit Uhr	*thy Watch*
Træet	*the Tree*
Mit Træe	*my Tree*

§ 38. In the Plural they are regular again, as

Singular		Plural
Brodet	*the Bread*	Dine Brod
Det Brod	*this Bread*	Disse Brod
Det Uhr	*thy Watch*	Dinè Uhr
Mit Træ	*my Tree*	Mine Træer

§ 39. All

§ 39. All Adjectives and some Substantives ending in EL ER, and EN, drop the E in the Plural Number, as

Singular	Plural
Gamel Ost	Gamle Oste
Old Cheese	*Old Cheeses*
En Skreven Bog	Skrevne Boger
A written Book	*The written Books*
Den bitter Viin	De bittre Viine
The bitter Wine	*The bitter Wines*
Himelen	Himlene
The Heaven	*The Heavens*
Et Væsen	De Væsner
A Substance	*The Substances*
Himeler	Himlerne
Heavens	*The Heavens*
Det Vaaben	De Vaabner
The Coat of Arms	*The Coat of Arms*

§ 40. Adjectives have always three Degrees of Comparison, *viz*

1. Positive. 2. Comparative. 3. Superlative.

§ 41. The Positive is the Single or Simple Sense or Meaning of a Word, as

    Smuk *Pretty*   Deilig *Handsome*

§ 42 The Comparative raises the Quality above what it is compared with, as

    Smukere *more Pretty* Deiligere *Handsomer*

§ 43. The

§ 43. The Superlative raises the Quality above both the former, to the highest Degree, as

Smukest *Prettiest*   Deiligst *Handsomest*

§ 44. The Comparative is for the most Part formed by adding RE, and the Superlative by EST.

Obs. The following Adjectives deviate from the Rules of the Degrees, and are irregular, as

Positive.	Comparat.	Superlat.
Faae	Færre	Færrest
few	*fewer*	*fewest*
Gamel	Ældre	Ældest
old	*older*	*oldest*
God	Bedre	Best
good	*better*	*best*
Lang	Længere	Længst
long	*longer*	*longest*
Liden	Mindre	Mindst
little	*less*	*least*
Mange	Flere	Flest
many	*more*	*most*
Megen	Mere	Mest
much	*more*	*most*
Ond	Verre	Verst
bad	*worse*	*worst*
Smaae	Smæere	Smæest
small	*less*	*least*
Stakked	Stækkere	Stækkest
short	*shorter*	*shortest*
Stor	Storre	Storst
great	*greater*	*greatest*
Ung	Yngere	Yngst
young	*younger*	*youngest*
Hoy	Hoyere	Hoyest
tall	*taller*	*tallest*

§ 45.

§ 45 There are also some Adverbs which fall under the same Observation.

Positive	Comparat.	Superlat
Bag		Bageſt
behind		*hindermoſt*
Fiern	Fierner	Fierneſt
far off	*farther off*	*fartheſt off*
Fore	Forre	Forreſt
before		*foremoſt*
Frem	Fremere	Fremeſt
forward	*more forward*	*moſt forward*
Gierne	Hellerer	Helſt
willingly	*more willingly*	*moſt willingly*
Ilde	Værrere	Værſt
ill	*worſe*	*worſt*
Inden	Indere	Indeſt
within	*further in*	*innermoſt*
Oven	Ovre	Overſt
above	*upper*	*uppermoſt*
Siden	Sidermere	Sidſt
afterward		
Tidt	Tiere	Tieſt
often	*oftener*	*ofteneſt*
Ude	Ydere	Ydeſt
out	*outer*	*outermoſt*
Unden	Undere	Underſt
under, below	*more under*	*undermoſt*
Vel	Bedre	Beſt
will	*better*	*beſt*

En

A general Table of the Danish Pronouns.

	Singularis.					Pluralis.		
	Nomin Vocat 1 Casus	Genetiv. 2 Casus	Dat. Acc. Abl 3 Casus			Nomen Voc 1 Casus	Genetiv. 2 Casus	Dat Acc. Abl 3 Casus
I Person	Ieg *I*	Min *my*	Mig *me*	1 Per.		Wi *we*	Vor *our*	Os *us*
II Person	Du *thou*	Din *thy*	Dig *thee*	2 Per.		I { *you* / *ye* }	Eders *your*	Eder *you*
III Person	Han *he*	Hans *his*	Ham *him*	3 Per.		De *they*	Deres *their*	Dem *them*
	Hun *she*	Hendes *hers*	Hende *her*					
	Det *it*	Dets *its*	Det *it*					
Relativa og Interrogativa	Hvo *who* Hvilken *which*	} Hvis *whose*	Hvem Hvilken	} *whom*		Hvilke *who or which*	Hvis *whose*	Hvilke *whom*
	Hvad *what*		Hvad					
	Som } *that* Der }		Som			Som } *that* Det }		Som *that*

Of Pronouns.

§ 46 Pronouns are used instead of Nouns, and are

1. Personal.

Singular		Plural	
Ieg	*I*	We *or* Man	*we*
Du	*thou*	I	*you*
Han	*he*	} De	*they*
Hun	*she*		

§ 47. Sing. Sing. Sing.

Dette or Denne } *this*	Hin *that*	Den *same* or the *same*
Plural	Plur.	Plur.
Disse *these*	Hine *those*	De *same* the *same*

§ 48. Relative.

Singular		
Hwilken	Der	Som
Plural		
Hvilke	De	Som

§ 49 Interogative.

Singular		
Hvo *or* Hvem	Hvilken	Hvad
Plural		
Hvo	Hvilke	Hvad

§ 50. Possessive

Singular		
Min	Sin	Din
Plural		
Mine	Sine	Dine

Of Verbs.

§ 51. The Verbs in Danish are as in other Languages, of different Kinds; what we shall make Observations on, are these following, *viz.*

1. Active.
2. Passive.
3. Neuter.
4. Reciprocal.
5. Irregular.

§ 52. The Active Verb expresses an Action, and necessarily implies an Agent, and an Object acted upon, as

Ieg Elsker *I love*
Ieg Elsker min Broder
I love my Brother

Here you see I is an Agent working with his Love upon the Object, *viz.* the Brother.

§ 53. The Passive Verb expresses Passion, Suffering, or the receiving of an Action, and necessarily implies an Object acted upon, as

At blive elsked *to be loved*
Min Broder er elsked of mig
My Brother is loved by me

Observ. Love is here the Passion, or receiving Action by my Brother, who is the Object my Love is shewn to, or works upon.

Christus er ofret for us
Christ is offered for us

> Ieg var fort tie Mile af ham
> *I was carried ten Miles by him*
>
> Doden er opfluget i Seyer
> *Death is swallowed up of Victory*
>
> Den sideste Fiende er Doden
> *The last Enemy is Death*
>
> Sejeren var Tilkiendet ham
> *The Victory is ascribed to him*

Obf. 1. When the Agent takes the Lead in the Sentence, the Verb is active

Obf. 2. When the Object takes the Lead, the Verb is passive, and is followed by the Agent.

§ 54. The Neuter Verb expresses a Being, when the Agent and Object acted upon coincide, and the Event is properly neither Action nor Passion, as

> Ieg har gaaet fra Borsen
> *I have walked from the Exchange*

Obf. Here you see Ieg is the Agent, and coincides with the Object (himself) that acts, or is acted on, and neither includes Action nor Passion.

> Hun har reist tre Mile
> *She has travelled three Miles*
>
> Barnet oversövede sig
> *The Child overslept himself*
>
> Manden har været i Arabien
> *The Man has been in Arabia*

§ 55. The

§ 55. The Reciprocal Verbs are when the Agent and Object acted upon, are the same, and carry

   Mig selv *Me myself*
   Sig selv *He himself*

Along with them, as

  At skaffe sig selv ret
   To right one's self

  At forsvære sig
   To forswear ones self

  At elske sig selv
   To love ones self

  Hun glæder sig selv
   She rejoices over herself

  Hun synes godt om sig selv
   She thinks well of herself

  Han giör sig færdig
   He makes himself ready

  Det sömer sig ikke
   It is not decent in itself

  Han fik hende til at troe sig
   He made her believe himself

  Han smigrer sig I Haabet
   He flatters himself in the Hope

  Han giör sig selv til Nar
   He makes himself a Fool

  Hun giftede sig til ham
   She married him

Hun retter fig efter fin Mand
She conforms herself to her Husband

Hun erinder fig felv
She remembers herself

§ 56. The Irregular Verbs are fo called, in refpect to the Tenfes, wherein they differ from the Regular.

Note, There are a great Number of them, and you will never be able to fpeak or write Danifh without learning them by heart, at leaft the Originals of them, as the Compofitives differ only in the Meaning according to the Prepofitions they are compounded with.

§ 57. The Danes and Englifh have moftly the fame Auxiliary Verbs, whereof thefe following are the moft principal, *viz*

1ft. At være *to be*

Indicative Mood.

Perfent	Ieg er	*I am*
Im-perf.	Ieg var	*I was*
Perf.	Ieg har været	*I have beeen*
Plu-perf.	Ieg havde været	*I had been*
Future	Ieg fkal or vil } være	*I fhall or will be*

Imperative.

Prefent	Vær Du		Lad ham være
	Be thou		*Let him be*
Future	Være fkall du		Være fkall De
	Thou fhalt be		*They fhall be*

2d. At

2d At have *to have*

Present	Ieg haver	*I have*
Im-perf.	Ieg havde	*I had*
Perfect.	Ieg haver haft	*I have had*
Postperf.	Ieg havde haft	*I had had*
Future	Ieg skall or vil } have	*I shall or will have*

§ 58. When you know how one Active Verb changes its Modes, Tenses and Persons, you know them all, and as the first Person is, so are the other Persons, *viz.*

Indicative Mood.

Present Tense.

Singular		Plural.	
Ieg elsker	*I love*	Vi Elsker	*we love*
Du	*thou love*	I	*you love*
Han	*he*	De	} *they*
Hun	*she*	De	

Imperfect.
Ieg elskede   *I loved*

Perfect.
Ieg har elsket   *I have loved*

Past-Perfect.
Ieg havde elsket   *I had loved*

Future.
Ieg skal elske   *I shall or will love*

Infinitive Mood.

Present	At elske	*To love*
Perf.	At have elsket	*To have loved*

Part.

Participle.
Elſkende — *Loving*

Supine.
Elſket — *Loved*

§ 59. The Paſſive Verb is likewiſe formed by the Auxiliary; at være *to be*, as

To be loved At være elſket

Paſſive.

Indicative Mood.

Preſent.
Ieg elſkes — *I am loved*

Imperfect.
Ieg er elſket — *I was loved*

Perfect.
Ieg har været elſket — *I have been loved*

Paſt-Perfect.
Ieg havde været elſked — *I had been loved*

Future
Ieg ſkall eller vil elſkes
I shall or *will be loved*

Infinitive.
Preſent. At elſkes *To be loved*

Participle.
Elſkendes — *Being loved*

Perfect Participle.
Er elſket — *Been loved*

Obſerv.

Obferv. Prefent Indicative
Future Indicative
Prefent Infinitive
Prefent Participle
Form their Paffive by S

Example.

	Active	Paffive
P. Indic.	Ieg tiener	Ieg tienes
	I ferve	*I am ferved*
F Indic.	Skal tiene	Skal tienes
	Shall ferve	*I fhall be ferved*
P. Infin.	At tiene	At tienes
	to ferve	*to be ferved*
P. Part	Tienende	Tienendes
	ferving	*being ferved*

§ 60 THE IRREGULAR VERBS, with their Compounds.

	Prefent.	Preter.	Particip.
To break	Bryder	Brod	Brudt
To break off	af bryder		
begin to trefpafs	and bryder		
break forth	for bryder		
through	frem bryder		
	gienem bryder	brod	brudt
in	ind bryder		
down	ned bryder		
to pieces	fonder bryder		
out	ud bryder		

(Compounds)

	Present.	Preter.	Part.
To command	Byder	Bod	Budet
forbid	for byder	⎫	
invite	ind byder	⎪	
undertake	mis byder	⎬ Compounds bod	budet
summon	op byder	⎪	
outbid one	over byder	⎪	
command	paa byder	⎪	
offer	til byder	⎪	
defy	ud byder	⎭	
To flow	Flyder	Flod	Flydt *and* Flodt
away	bort flyder	⎫	
in	ind flyder	⎪	
about	om flyder	⎬ flod	flydt
over	over flyder	⎪	
to	til flyder	⎪	
out	ud flyder	⎭	
To repent	Fortryder	Fortrodt	Fortrodt *and* Fortrydt
To climb	Klyver	Klov	Klovet
away	bort klyver		
up	op klyver		
over	over klyver		
To creep	Kryber	Krob	Kkrobet *and* Krybet
through	giennem kryber	⎫	
in	ind kryber	⎪	
down	ned kryber	⎬ krob	krybet
up	op kryber	⎪	
over	over kryber	⎪	
out	ud kryber	⎭	

To the DANISH LANGUAGE.

	Present	Preter.	Part
To flake	Fyger	Fog	Foget
rage, fret or foam	fnyfer	fnos	fnoft
frighten	kyfer	kos	kofet and kyfet
grumble	knyger	knog	knyget
get, enjoy	nyder	nod	nydt
lye	lyver be lyver paa lyver	loy	loyet
To flee or fly	Flyver	Floy	Floyet
fly away	bort flyver		
in	ind flyver		
down	ned flyver	floy	floyet
over	over flyver		
out	ud flyver		
To shoot, or push	Skyder	Skod	Skydet and Skudt
discharge	af skyder		
combat	be skyder		
advance	fore skyder		
push from	fra skyder	skod	
forth	frem skyder		
down	ned skyder		
out	red skyder		
To reject	for skyder		
To snot the nose	Snyder	Snodt	Snydt and Snodt
brag	skryder	skrod	skrydet and skrodt
boil	fyder	fodt	fydet

To

40 A Short INTRODUCTION

	Present	Preter.	Part.
To strike plain	Stryger	Strog	Stroget *and* Stryget
off	af stryger	} strog	
	and stryger		
in	be stryger		
away	bort stryger		
over	over stryger		
on	paa stryger		
out	ud stryger		
To freeze	Fryser	Fros	Froset
off	af fryser	} fros	froset
away	bort fryser		
through	gennem fryser		
over	over fryser		
together	samen fryser		
To ask, or *beg*	Beder	Bad	Bedet
excuse	af beder	} bad	bedet
adore	til beder		
solicit	om beder		
beg	ud beder		
To ride	Rider	Red	Rider
manage a horse	be rider	} red	ridet
ride away	bort rider		
forth	hen rider		
in	ind rider		
over	over rider		
out	ud rider		
To tear	River	Rev	Revet
tear off	af river	} rev	revet
away	bort river		
down	ned river		

To

To the DANISH LANGUAGE.

	Present	Præt.	Part.
To tear up	op river	} rev	revet
asunder	sonder river		
out	ud river		
To slide	Skrider	Skreed	Skridt
slide away	bort skrider		
in	ind skrider		
to	til skrider		
To cry	Skriger	Skreg	Skreget
call	and skriger		
lament for	be skriger		
cry out after	efter skriger		
out-cry one	over skriger		
cry out	ud skriger		
To take fire	Svider	Sved	Svidet
To wear	Slider	Sled	Slede
wear off, tear off	af slider		
consume	bort slider		
waste	for slider		
To sneak	Sniger	Sneg	Sniget
secretly	hen sniger		
in	ind sniger		
out	und sniger		
deceive	be sniger		
To rise or mount	Stiger	Steg	Steget
mount	be stiger		
dismount	af stiger		
mount forth	and stiger		
after	efter stiger		
descend	ned stiger		
mount up	op stiger		
over	over stiger		
out	ud stiger		

To

	Present	Pret.	Part
To *write*	Skriver	Skrev	Skievet
copy	af skriver		
describe	be skriver		
transcribe	efter skriver		
command	for skriver		
prescribe	fore skriver		
write to	hen skriver		
inscribe	ind skriver		
To *deceive*	Sviger	Sveg	Sveget
cheat	be sviger		
To *bite*	Bider	Bed	Bidt
bite off	af bider		
bite	and bider		
bite through	giennem bider		
bite in	ind bider		
To *abide*	Bliver	Blev	Blevet
stay, tarry	for bliver		
stay by	hos bliver		
To *drive*	Driver	Drev	Drevet
commit	be driver		
drive away	bort driver		
expel	for driver		
refute	igien driver		
drive through	igien driver		
about	hen driver		
in	ind driver		
about	om driver		
together	samen driver		
To *say, or tell*	Siger	Sagde	Sagt
renounce	af siger		
dictate	fore siger		
contradict	imod siger		

TO THE DANISH LANGUAGE. 43

	Present	Pret.	Part.
To unsay	op siger	sagde	sagt
promise	til siger		
depose	ud siger		
To give	Giver	Gav	Givet
deliver	af giver		
declare, impeach	and giver		
come to pass	be giver		
give away	bort giver		
yield	efter giver		
pardon	for giver		
give out, pretend	fore giver		
deliver	frem giver		
inspire	ind giver		
encompass	om giver		
give up	op giver		
resign	over giver		
pardon	til giver		
distribute, spend	ud giver		
To know	Veed	Vidste	Vidst
To suffer	Lider	Leed	Lidet
To tread	Triner	Tren	Trinet
To smite	Smider	Smed	Smidet
away	bort smider		
out	hen smider		
down	ned smider		
about	om smider		
over	over smider		
on	paa smider		
to	til smider		
To sing	Synger	Sang	Sunget

To

44 A Short INTRODUCTION

	Present	Pret.	Part.
To sink	Synker	Sank	Synket
go to the bottom	for synker		
sink down	hen synker		
in	ind synker		
down	ned synker		
To slip	Sliper	Slap	Slupet
away	bort sliper		
in	ind sliper		
down	ned sliper		
out	ud sliper		
To spin	Spinder	Spandt	Spundet
up	op spinder		
out	ud spinde		
To leap, spring	springer	Sprang	Sprunget
leap off	af springer		
away	bort springer		
after	efter springer		
from	frem springer		
through	igiennem springer		
in	ind springer		
down	ned springer		
up	op springer		
over	over springer		
out	ud springer		
To sting, wound	Stikker	Stak	Stukket
pitch	af stikker		
set on fire	and stikker		
corrupt, bribe	be stikker		
pocket up	ind stikker		
open a bill	op stikker		
ingrave	ud stikker		

To the DANISH LANGUAGE.

	Present	Pret. Part
To shrink	Svinder	Svandt Svindet
up	op svinder	
in	ind svinder	
To bind, or *tie*	Binder	Bandt Bundet
with a rope	and binder	
one up	for binder	
tie up	op binder	
together	sammen binder	
To drink	Drikker	Drak Drukket
out	ud drikker	
in	in drikker	
to	til drikker	
To find	Finder	Fandt Fundet
find	be finder	
invent	op finder	
invent	paa finder	
find out	ud finder	
To run, or *flow*	Rinder	Randt Rundet
off	af rinder	
away	bort rinder	
down	ned rinder	
out	ud rinder	
up	op rinder	
To sit	Sidder	Sad Siddet
possess	be sidder	
sit down	ned sidder	
To swing	Svinger	Svang Svinget
To constrain, force	} Tvinger	Tvang Tvunget
force	af tvinger	
force out	ud tvinger	

46   A Short INTRODUCTION

	Present	Pret.	Part
To sting	Stinger	Stang	Stunget
To win, gain	Vinder	Vandt	Vundet
gain from	fra vinder		
gain over	over vinder		
To witness	Vidner	Vandt	Vidnet
testify	be vidner		
To lye, lay down	Ligger	Laa	Ligget
To bring	Bringer	Bragte	Bragt
accommodate	and bringer		
carry away	bort bringer		
bring forth	frem bringer		
propose	fore bringer		
bring again	gien bringer		
To burst	Brister	Brast	Brustet
To eat	Æder	Aad	Ædt
eat up	op æder		
through	giennem æder		
out	ud æder		
To be	Være	Var	Været
have no need of	und være		
To help	Hielper	Hialp	Hiulpet
make shift with	be hielper		
raise up	op hielper		
to	til h elper		
out	ud hielper		

To

To the DANISH LANGUAGE.

	Present	Pret.	Part.
To carry, or *bear*	Bærer	Bar	Baaret
carry away	bort bærer		
forth	frem bærer		
along	hen bærer		
in	in bærer		
about	om bærer		
up	op bærer		
over	over bærer		
out	ud bærer		
To cut, or *carve*	Skiærer	Skar	Skaaret
cut off	af skiærer		
round	be skiærer		
through	giennem skiærer		
about	om skiærer		
up	op skiærer		
over	over skiærer		
carve	ud skiæder		
To steal	Stiæler	Stial	Stiaalet
rob	be stiæler		
enlist	ind stiæler		
steal out	ud stiæler		
To tread	Træder	Traad	Traadet
retire	af træder		
enter upon	be træder		
tread down	bort træder		
forth	frem træder		
under	under træder		
injure	for træder		
tread in	ind træder		
amongst	imellem træder		
over	over træder		
accede	til træder		
go out	ud træder		

48   A Short INTRODUCTION

	Present	Pret	Part
To perceive	Fornemer	Fornam	Fornumet
To help	Hielper	Hialp	Hiulpet
enable	be hielper		
raise up	op hielper		
assert	til hielper		
to help out	ud hielper		
To reach	Rekker	Rakte	Rakt
hand one a thing	til rekker		
stretch out	ud rekker		
To awake	Vækker	Vakte	Vakt
To pull or draw	Trækker	Trak	Trækket
pull off	af trækker		
cover, or cheat	be trækker		
pull forward	frem trækker		
through	giennem trækker		
in	ind trækker		
about	om trækker		
also	op trækker		
to	til trækker		
out	ud trækker		
To hit	Treffer	Traf	Truffen
hit on	and treffer		
regard	be treffer		
happen	ind treffer		
happen	til treffer		
To be worth	Gielder	Galdt	Giældet
respect	and gielder		
reward	giennem gielder		
make one suffer	und gielder		

To

To the DANISH LANGUAGE.

	Present	Pret.	Part.
To lay	Lægger	Lagde	Lagt
off	af lægger		
a plan	and lægger		
incumber	be lægger		
lay before	frem lægger		
off	fra lægger		
aside	hen lægger		
in	ind lægger		
down	ned lægger		
over	over lægger		
on	paa lægger		
together	samen lægger		
to	til lægger		
out	ud lægger		
reward	veder lægger		
To found	Knæller	Kald	Knaldt
To thresh	Tærsker	Tarsk	Tærsket
thresh off	af tærsker		
out	ud tærsker		
To set	Sætter	Sadt	Sadt
off	af sætter		
upon	and sætter		
beset	be sætter		
pursue	efter sætter		
propose	frem sætter		
set aside	hen sætter		
by	hos sætter		
against	imod sætter		
in	ind sætter		
down	ned sætter		
up	op sætter		
together	samen sætter		

50 A Short INTRODUCTION

	Present	Pret.	Part.
To set to	til sætter		
set out	ud sætter		
translate	over sætter		
assist	und sætter		
To count	Tæller	Talte	Talt
count off	af tæller		
after	efter tæller		
again	om tæller		
sum up	op tæller		
count over	over tæller		
count to	til tæller		
till	for tæller		
count out	ud tæller		
To scold	Skiælder	Skieldte	Skieldet
chide	over skiælder		
blame one	ud skiælder		
To sell	Sælger	Saalte	Saalt
off	af sælger		
away	bort sælger		
to	til sælger		
out	ud sælger		
To draw	Drager	Drog	Draget
off	af drager		
put on	and drager		
deceive	be drager		
go abroad	bort drager		
prefer	fore drager		
draw forth	frem drager		
in	ind drager		
about	om drager		
over	over drager		
up	op drager		

To

To the DANISH LANGUAGE. 51

	Present	Pret.	Part.
To draw to	til drager		
out	ud drager		
escape	und drager		
To fare	Farer	Foer	Faret
depart	bort farer		
experience	for farer		
draw off	hen farer		
descend	ned farer		
trawl about	om farer		
ascend	op farer		
go into	ind farer		
go to	til farer		
be repaid	veder farer		
To chase	Jager	Jog	Jaget
drive away	bort jager		
pursue	efter jager		
drive forth	hen jager		
hunt in	ind jager		
about	om jager		
up	op jager		
together	samen jager		
out	ud jager		
To dig	Graver	Grov	Gravet
bury	be graver		
dig through	igiennem graver		
in	ind graver		
about	om graver		
up	op graver		
out	ud graver		
To crow	Galer	Goel	Galet

	Present	Pret.	Part.
To take	Tager	Tog	Taget
take off	af tager		
accept	and tager		
prevent	be tager		
deprive	bort tager		
undertake	fore tager		
mistake	for tager		
repeat	gien tager		
take away	hen tager		
receive	imod tager		
be fond of, *take in*	ind tager		
borrow	op tager		
grow	til tager		
take out	ud tager		
except	und tager		
confirm	ved tager		
To hide	Dölger	Dulgte	Dölget
conceal	for dolger		or Dulgt
To follow	Folger	Fulgte	Fulgt
follow out	bort folger		
after	efter folger		
pursue	for folger		
attend one	hen folger		
succeed	paa folger		
To ask	Sporger	Spurgte	Spurgt
interrogate	ad sporger		
consult	be sporger		
enquire	efter spörger		
ask for	fore spörger		
	op sporger		
question	til sporger		
examine	ud sporger		

To

TO THE DANISH LANGUAGE.

	Present	Pret.	Part.
To smear	Smorer	Smurte	Smurt
To be constrained	Bor	Burde	Burdet
To make, or *do*	Gior	Giorde	Giort
settle	af gior		
imitate	efter gior		
alter	om gior		
trespass	for gior		
offend	imod gior		
make out	ud gior		
To dare	Tor	Torde	Tordt
To weigh	Veyer	Vog	Veyet
Can	Kand	Kunde	Kundet
To come	Kommer	Kom	Kommet
arrive	and komer		
receive	be komer		
execute	efter komer		
come forward	frem komer		
prevent	fore komer		
destroy }	om komer		
	for komer		
come in	ind komer		
up	op komer		
over	over komer		
out	ud komer		
belong to	ved komer		
To run	Lober	Lob	Lobet
run against	and lober		
eperience	be lober		
run away	bort lober		
after	efter lober		
	for lober		

H

54 A Short INTRODUCTION

	Present	Pret	Part.
To run forth	hen lober		
in	ind lober		
about	om lober		
over	over lober		
together	samen lober		
to	til lober		
escape	und lober		
run out	ud lober		
To sleep	Sover	Sov	Sovet
lay with a girl	besover		
over sleep	for sover		
sleep in	hen sover		
sleep by	hos sover		
fall asleep	ind sover		
sleep out	ud sover		
To get, obtain	Faar	Fik	Faaet
To go, or walk	Gaaer	Gik	Gaaet
go away	af gaar		
regard	and gaar		
commit	be gaar		
go away	bort gaar		
after	efter gaar		
vanish	for gaar		
proceed	fore gaar		
proceed	frem gaar		
return	gien gaar		
go abroad	hen gaar		
in	ind gaar		
about	om gaar		
excell	over gaar		
accede	til gaar		
go out	ud gaar		

To

To the DANISH LANGUAGE.

	Present	Preter.	Part.
To *escape*	und gaar		
confess, or *confirm*	ved gaar		
To *beat*	Slaar	Slog	Slaget
beat off	af flaar		
fix or *pin*	and flaar		
	be flaar		
project	fore flaar		
beat through	giennem flaar		
down	ned flaar		
knock up	up flaar		
To *beat*	Slaar	Slog	Slaget
calculate	over flaar		
happen	til flaar		
beat out	ud flaar		
excuse	und flaar		
beat under	under flaar		
To *stand*	Staar	Stod	Staaet
desist	af staar		
become	and staar		
consist	be staar		
assist	bie staar		
stand after	efter staar		
understand	for staar		
administer	fore staar		
resist	imod staar		
insist	paa staar		
rise, or *stand up*	op staar		
stand to	til staar		
suffer	ud staar		
dare	under staar		

To

	Present	Pret	Past
To laugh	Leer	Loe	Leet
deride	be leer		
	ud Leer		
To see, or *look*	Seer		
contemplate	an seer		
	be seer		
look after	efter seer		
provide	for seer		
look through	giennem seer		
be ashamed	und seer		
look about	om seer		
	op seer		
	over seer		
	til seer		
	ud seer		
To be silent	Tier	Taug	Tiet
conceal	for		
keep silent	stiltier		

As in the ENGLISH GRAMMAR you have learned, what is to be understood by Adverbs, Conjunctions, Propositions and Interjections, and there is nothing materially different from the DANISH, I shall leave them all to the Exercise of your Memory, and after adding two Remarks on Adverbs, shall treat a little on the Composition of Single Words and the Syntax.

1. When an Adverb has its Derivation from an Adjective, that terminates in Lig, as Venlig: Friendly it assumes EN, as Venligen.

2. If

2. If the Adjective does not end in Lig, the Adverb is made of it by adding a T, as Smuk, *Pretty*, Smukt.

On the Composition of single Words in a Sentence, and their Construction.

§ 1. The Articles determine the different Signification of Nouns.

§ 2. The Articles are either of Unity, or Definitive

§ 3. The Definitive is again, either Pre *or* Post } Positive.

§ 4. We must also observe, when these are used, and when not.

§ 5. It it not used,

1. When the Nouns are in an Indefinite Sense, as

  Fuld af Sorrig
  Full of Sorrow

  Mange Penger
  Enough of Money

2. When the Nouns carry an Adjective before them, or a Possessive Pronoun, as

  Bliv ved friskt Moed
  Be of good Spirit

  Elsk din Hustrue
  Love thy Wife

3 When the Nouns are Proper Nouns, as London, John.

> John reiste til Paris
> *John went to Paris*

4. When the Nouns stand in the Genitive, as

> Mandens Daarlighed
> *The Foolishness of Man*
>
> Retferdiheds Beromelse
> *The Honour of Justice*

§ 6. On all other Occasions the Nouns have their Article before them, viz either Unitatis, or the Indefinite, as

> Et Hüüs, *a House*, that is, *any House*

§ 7 Or Definitive, which is used as the English The, as

> Den Mand *The Man*

That is, *Some one Man in particular*

> Manden *The Man*

§ 8 These Articles, the Nouns make use of, although an Adjective is put before them.

> Den gode Mand
> *The good Man*
>
> En god Mand
> *A good Man*

§ 9. The Definitive Article is either Pre or Post Positive.

Observe, That the Postpositive doth not encompass or limit the Sense of the Words so much as the Prepositive.

§ 10. The

§ 10. The Prepositive is more particular in its Determination, and is used on the following Occasions, *viz.*

1. When the Noun has an Adjective before it, as

>Den store Kiærlighed
>*The great Love.*

Not Kierligheden stor, *or* stor Kiæligheden.

2. Before a Noun which is followed by a Relative Pronoun,

>Den Mand som elsker
>*The Man who loves*

>Den Lykke som I har
>*The Luck which you have*

§ 11. On all other Occasions the Postpositive is used as the English Definite Article. The, as

>Kierlighedens Fader
>*Father of the Love*

>Froen til Saligheden
>*The Faith to the Salvation*

§ 12. The Adjective is always put before the Substantive.

>Det andet Aar
>*The second Year*

§ 13 The Adjective is unaltered although the Substantive is of the Genitive Case

>Den Tappere Soldats Berömelse
>*The Honour of the good Soldier*

§ 14. If an Adjective is put in the Genitive Case it stands by itself as a Substantive, and its Substantive Noun is to be understood as wanted, or to be there in reality.

 De Lærdes Strid er heftig
 The War of the learned (Men) is great

§ 15. When two Substantives come together, signifying the same Thing, they are both put in the same Case, as

 En Hob Mennesker
 A Multitude of People

 Broder George
 Brother George

 De approrere Joderne
 The rebellious Jews.

§ 16 If two or more Nouns speak of different Things, or the one denotes a Possession, the Possession Word is put in the Genitive Case, as

 Broder Georgs Skrivelse
 The Letter of Brother George

 Den Tappre Heltés Levent
 The Life of the victorious Hero

 En Konges Son. *Son of a King.*

§ 17. The Noun in the Genitive Case stands always before the Noun that Causes its Termination.

 De Danskes Cappel
 The Chapel of the Danes

 Den store Herres Vaaben
 The Coat of Arms of the Great Lord.

§ 18.

§ 18. Words by way of Question and Answer, require one and the same Case.

>Quest. Hvo taler? *Who speaks?*
>Answ *Paul speaks.*
>Quest Hvis Kiortel er Denne?
>Answ. *Peter's or my Brother George's Coat.*

Except. The Interrogative Pronoun as well as the Pronoun we make answer with, are both put in the Dative Case.

>Quest Hvem er Det? *Who is it?*
>Answ. Mig or Det er mig *I, or it is I.*

Of a Participle.

§ 19. A Participle is not only like an Adjective, and made use of in the same Manner, but partakes also of the Nature of a Verb in Conjugation and Tenses, as

>Han Svarde Sigendes
>*He answered and said*

Obs. 1. No Period must begin with a Participle.

Obs. 2. After the Imperfect Tense the Participle is often used, as

>Han rejste sig op sigende
>*He arose saying*

>At han vilde fegtende forsvare
>*That he would, fighting, defend*

>Sit Bytte, Der Kom fra Lejeren
>*His Spoil which came from the Field of Battle*

I

Led-

Ledsagendes af et Partie Ryttere
And was convoyed by a Party of Dragoons.

§ 20. The Compound Verbs are mostly separated from their Prepositions when they are put in a Sentence, so that the Simple Verb comes first; then the Case, which such Verb governs, and after that the Proposition, which before was joined to the Verb, as

Han har lagt Penger op
He has laid up Money
Instead of
Han har oplagt Penger
He has uplaid Money

Han har staaet hende bie
Det komer hende ikke ved

Obs. 1. They seldom undergo this Separation in the Present Participle.

2. Some Verbs are compounded of Prepositions that cannot be separated, as Be, En, ge, mis, u, und.

    Bestaae   *Consist*
    Mishage *Displeasure*
    Undgaae *Evitable.*

§ 21 The Tenses are all the same as in English, and are made use of in the same Manner, and need no particular Observation, but that the Person stands often behind the Simple Tense of the Verb, and also between the Auxiliary Verb, and the Supine in Compound Verbs, as

  Har han det *Has he that*
  Har han faaet det *Has he got it*
  Saa havde han skrevet *So had he wrote.*

§ 22.

§ 22 When two Verbs come together, the laſt is put in the Infinitive Mood, with at *as*

 Han har at ſkrive *He has to write*
 Hun lover at ſynge *She promiſes to ſing*

Of Adverbs.

When an Adverb ſtands by a Noun, it is always put before it, as

  Særdeles Stor
  Eſpecially large

§ 23. With Verbs it ſtands directly before, or directly after, and likewiſe in the compound Tenſes between the Auxiliary Verb and the Supine, and alſo after the Caſe which the Verb governs.

§ 24 When it ſtands with a compound Verb, it is put between it and the Prepoſition, as

  Han har ſtaaet mig trolig bie
  He has aſſiſted me truly

  Han vil rejſe ſnart bort
  He will go ſoon away

Of Prepositions.

§ 25. A Prepoſition ſtands always before its Noun; but if a Sentence begins with ſuch a Word that has a Prepoſition, then the Prepoſition parts with the Noun, and takes its Place in the End of the Period, as

  Hlvem vil I tale ved
  Whom will you ſpeak with.

Per

Perſonen ſom vi rejſte med
The perſon we traveled with

§ 26 All the Prepoſitions govern an Accuſative Caſe except Til Inden, uden, which ſometimes govern a Genitive, as

    Til Fods   Uden Lands
    By Foot   *In foreign Country*

    Inden Dors   *Within Doors*

Of Conſtruction.

§ 27. The Conjunction with the Nominative Caſe ſtands always before the Verb.

§ 28. The Gerund (which is the indefinitive Mood with a Propoſition before it) follows the Verb which it is governed by.

§ 29. Next the Verb follows the Caſe which the Verb governs.

§ 30. The auxiliary Verb ſtands always before the Verb it is joined with

§ 31 The Infinitive Mood follows the Verb which it is governed by, and the Prepoſition before its Caſe

Note The Genitive Caſe, as well as the Adjective, ſtands always before its Subſtantive.

On

On the Construction of a Sentence, the following will serve as an Example.

1. The Conjunction.
Hvis, ikkun

2. The Nominative with its Conjunction.
Den kloge Konges i Macedonien Philippi tappre Son, Alexander den Store.

3. The first auxiliary Verb.
Havde.

4. The Adverb.
Ofte nok.

5. The second auxiliary Verb.
Vil det.

6. The Verb itself.
Erindre.

7. The reciprocal Pronoun.
Sig.

8. The Case of the Verb.
Sin kloge Læreres. Grund Regler.

9. The Gerund with its Connection.
I at bruge sine Kræfter og de ting han besad.

10. The first Preposition with its Case.
Efter sin beste Indsigt.

11. The second Preposition.
Til sin og andres Velfærds Befordrelse.

Hvis ikkun, den kloge Konges i Macedonien Phi-
if   but   wise   King   Macedon
lippi tappre Søn, Alexander den store havde
victorious Son   great   have
ofte nok vildet erindre sig sin kloge Læreres
often enough will remember see his witty Tutor
Grund-Regler, i at bruge sine Kræfter og de
fundamental Rule   use   Parts
Ting han besad efter sin beste Indsigt til sin
Thing   possess   best   Judgment
og andres Velfærds Befordrelse.
other Welfare Promotion.

EXAMPLE.
Skulde denne korte Indledelse til det Danske
Sprog blve til Nytte for mine smaae Venner, hvis
Tieneste den egentlig er sigtet til og tillige finde
andres Biefald, vil det blive enfærdeles Fornoy-
else til Forfateren.

If this short Introduction should be of Service
to my little Friends, for whose Use it is chiefly
intended, and also meet with the Approbation of
others, it will be a great Pleasure to the Com-
piler.

FINIS.

To be Corrected.

PAGE 5 line 12 for indifinite, read indefinite
——————— 14 indifinite, r. indefinite
Page 6 l. 12 and 17, Tomfru, r. Jomfrue Jomfruer
Page 7 l. 13 Brod r. Bröd
Page 8 l. 20 Ford r. Jord
Page 9 l. 32 anfight r. anfigt
Page 10 l. 8 Baronie r. Baronie
——————— 31 Borgefkab r. Borgerfkab
Page 12 l. 6 Fongfel r. Fængfel
——————— 9 Folgefkab r. Fölgefkab
——————— 24 Foll r. Föl
——————— 26 Forgtft r. Forgift
——————— 29 Fyztoy r. Fyrtöy
Page 13 l. 19 Harnifh r. Harnifk
Page 15 l. 12 Loft r. Loft
Page 16 l. 21 Politic r. Politie
Page 17 l. 9 Rüs-papir r. Ruspapir
——————— 13 Ris r. Rus
Page 19 l. 13 Senge, Tepen r. Senge-Teppen
——————— 16 Snore, Liv r. Snöre-Liv
Page 20 l. 7 Verfe r Vers
——————— 13 Veyer r. Vejer
——————— 26 Plight r. Pligt
Page 22 l. 15 Tongue r. Tong
Page 23 l. 23 Oxen r. Oxen
Page 27 l 29 Stôr r. Stor
Page 31 l. 22 elfked of mig r elked af mig
Page 32 l. 6 Sidefte Fiende r Sidfte Fiende
Page 36 l 13 Ieg er elfket r. Ieg var elfked
Page 39 l. 23 red fkyder r. udfkyder
Page 40 l. 21 part. Rider r redet
Page 41 l. 16 part. Slede r. Sledet
Page 42 l. 25 igien driver r. igiennem driver
Pfige 47 l. 18 ud fkiæder r. udfkiærer
Page 55 l. 11 up flaar r. opflaar
Page 56 l. 5 Seer perf. r. Saae part. Seet

Printing in General neatly and expeditiously performed, by

R. HILTON,

PRINTER and BOOKSELLER, No. 8, Well-close Square, near Ratcliff Highway, LONDON;

Where may be had, Price 6s. sewed,

A View of all Religions in the World, with the several Church Governments from the Creation to the present Times, and choice Observations and Reflections throughout the Whole. Written in the Year 1640, by ALEXANDER ROSS, Chaplain in Ordinary to King Charles the First, and brought down to the present Times by a late eminent Clergyman of the Church of England; brought up in the Jesuit's College at Lisbon, but renouncing the Errors of Rome, became a distinguished Member of the Reformed Church.

CPSIA information can be obtained at www.ICGtesting.com
Printed in the USA
LVOW03s1518240414

383118LV00018B/430/P